Be Positive...
Be Happy

Inspiring Words to
Color Your Outlook
on Life

A Blue Mountain Arts® Collection

Blue Mountain Press™
Boulder, Colorado

We wish to thank Susan Polis Schutz for permission to reprint the following poems that appear in this publication: "Find happiness in nature…." Copyright © 1983 by Stephen Schutz and Susan Polis Schutz. And for "This life is yours…." Copyright © 1979 by Continental Publications. All rights reserved. And PrimaDonna Entertainment Corp. for "Wake up every day…" and "You have power over your thoughts…" by Donna Fargo. Copyright © 2004, 2005 by PrimaDonna Entertainment Corp. And Jason Blume for "When the challenges that lie ahead…." Copyright © 2015 by Jason Blume. All rights reserved.

ISBN: 978-1-68088-178-3

Printed in China.
First Printing: 2017

Blue Mountain Arts, Inc.
P.O. Box 4549, Boulder, Colorado 80306

Introduction

The beneficial effects of positive thinking are well documented. An upbeat attitude favorably impacts every aspect of life — work, health, relationships, and general well-being. It expands your view of what is possible, making it easier to approach life's difficulties and challenges. By looking on the bright side, you create a better environment for yourself as well as for those around you.

Coloring has been shown to relieve stress, improve mood, and increase concentration. This simple escape from the hectic pace of daily life provides a chance to slow down, relax, and tap into your deepest inner thoughts. You will feel calm, rested, and ready to take on whatever comes your way.

Put positive thinking and coloring together and you have this unique coloring book — a perfect combination of inspiration and imagination. We suggest that you start by reading some of the thoughtful messages that accompany the illustrations throughout this book. With those words in mind, choose a design that speaks to you. You don't have to be an artist to create a masterpiece —

just use the colors and art supplies that represent your preferences and personality. Some days you might feel a bit more grounded and want to color the sky blue and the grass green. Other days you may feel more like a dreamer who's wondering what the world would look like if the sun were purple and the clouds were orange. Let your feelings guide you, and let the words inspire you to make each page your own.

Use this coloring book as a tool for meditation and reflection, a place for artistic expression, or just a fun activity where you can invite friends or family to join in. Spending time coloring can start your morning on a happy note, give you a much-needed break from your full schedule during the day, or help you unwind when you get home at night. So open up your favorite pack of coloring supplies, take a deep breath, and begin.

Happy Coloring!

Take a moment to look around and smile at your life and your choices. Don't worry about the paths you should have taken or the opportunities you ignored. Instead, breathe in the life that surrounds you — let it fill your soul with light and hope. Reflect on the past and all the memories, good and bad, that have made you who you are today. Your journey is far from over, as you will continue to grow, change, and flourish.

Take a moment *every* day to think positive thoughts.

Carol Schelling

Yesterday is behind you. What's done is done, and it's important to take what you've learned from the experience and just move on.

Today is a brand-new opportunity, a blank canvas, an unwritten page in the diary. All that needs to happen right now is for you... to do the amazing things you're capable of.

And tomorrow? That's the place where promises come true. Just remember... you can't change a single thing about the past, but you can change absolutely everything about the future.

⁓

Douglas Pagels

Joy is
not in things;
it is in us.

— Richard Wagner

You have power over your thoughts and feelings. Don't let your circumstances dictate how you feel. Don't let your thoughts and feelings color your situation blue or desperate.

Decide that life is good and you are special. Decide to enjoy today. Decide that you will live life to the fullest now, no matter what. Trust that you will change what needs changing, but also decide that you're not going to put off enjoying life just because you don't have everything you want now. Steadfastly refuse to let anything steal your joy. Choose to be happy... and you will be!

≈

Donna Fargo

Believe

What is most important is not
    where you stand,
but the direction you're going in.
It's more than never having bad moments;
it's knowing you are always
    bigger than the moment.
It's believing you have already
    been given everything
you need to handle life.
It's the belief in your heart
    that there will always be
more good than bad in the world.

Vickie M. Worsham

This life is yours
Take the power
to choose what you want to do
and do it well
Take the power
to love what you want in life
and love it honestly
Take the power
to walk in the forest
and be a part of nature
Take the power
to control your own life
No one else can do it for you
Take the power
to make your life
healthy
exciting
worthwhile
and very happy

≈

Susan Polis Schutz

When the challenges that lie ahead
seem too great to bear
and you don't know where you will get
the strength to carry on,
you will find a well of strength and courage
you never imagined you possessed.

With faith, love, and support,
you can walk through even the greatest trial.
Trust that you will have all you need
to get through hard times, and remember...
you need only face one day at a time.

— Jason Blume

You have a chance to be as happy as any one person has ever been. You have an opportunity to be as proud as anyone you've ever known. You have the potential to make a very special dream come true.

And all you have to do... is recognize the possibilities, the power, and the wonder of... today.

Douglas Pagels

© BMA, Inc.

Trust your decisions and feelings
and do what is best for you.
Don't let anyone else's negativity
influence your dreams, values,
or hopes.
Focus on what you can change
and let go of what you can't.
Concentrate on the positives
and combine faith with
generous portions of patience
and determination.
Step boldly and confidently
into your future
where happiness, success,
and dreams await you.

≈

Barbara Cage

you Are
what you
Think
you Are

You will be whatever you resolve to be.
Determine to be something in the world,
and you will be something.

"I cannot," never accomplished anything.

But "I will try," has worked wonders.

— ⁓ —

Joel Hawes

Most of the shadows of this life are caused by standing in one's own sunshine.

— Ralph Waldo Emerson

Finish every day and be done with it. You have done what you could. Some blunders and absurdities no doubt crept in; forget them as soon as you can. Tomorrow is a new day; begin it well and serenely and with too high a spirit to be cumbered with your old nonsense. This day is all that is good and fair. It is too dear, with its hopes and invitations, to waste a moment on the yesterdays.

Ralph Waldo Emerson

Living life as a positive person means living a life that is blessed with awareness, appreciation, and accomplishment.

When you are a positive person, there is always a brighter light in your life. More goals get reached and more journeys take you exactly where you want to go. You can add immensely to your serenity and your opportunities can blossom more beautifully.

When you have hope in your heart and a great attitude, you can live with an abundance of goodness and grace shining inside you.

Douglas Pagels

There is one kind of laugh that I always did recommend; it looks out of the eye first with a merry twinkle, then it creeps down on its hands and knees and plays around the mouth like a pretty moth around the blaze of a candle, then it steals over into the dimples of the cheeks and rides around in those whirlpools for a while, then it lights up the whole face like the mellow bloom on a damask rose, then it swims up on the air, with a peal as clear and as happy as a dinner-bell, then it goes back again on gold tiptoes like an angel out for an airing, and it lies down on its little bed of violets in the heart where it came from.

Josh Billings

Refuse
to Be
Unhappy

Refuse to dwell on the mistakes
    or disappointments
that are sometimes a part of life;
instead learn how you can
    make things better.
Be optimistic.
Be energetic and positive
    about the things you do,
and always hope for the best.

≈

Ben Daniels

It is never too late to be what you might have been.

— George Eliot

Knowing in your heart that you are in charge of your destiny can give you the power to overcome obstacles. It's an attitude that carries you through the tough times and that looks at the positives and defies the negatives.

—

Barbara Cage

If you want to be healthy morally, mentally, and physically, just let go. Let go of the little annoyances of everyday life, the irritations and the petty vexations that cross your path daily. Don't take them up, nurse them, pet them, and brood over them. They are not worthwhile. Let them go!

Learn to let go. As you value health of body and peace of mind, let go — just simply let go!

Author Unknown

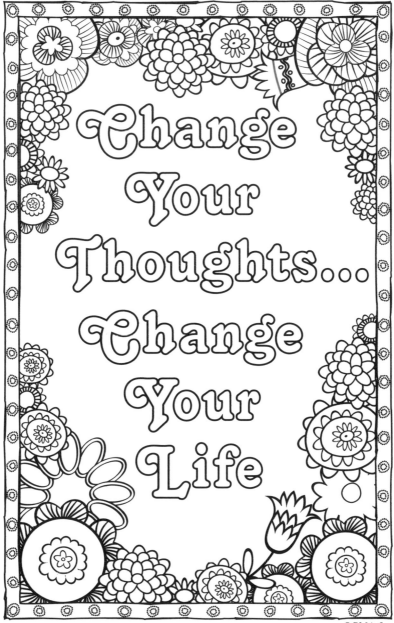

I am convinced that attitude is the key to success or failure in almost any of life's endeavors. Your attitude — your perspective, your outlook, how you feel about yourself, how you feel about other people — determines your priorities, your actions, your values. Your attitude determines how you interact with other people and how you interact with yourself.

Caroline Warner

Open new doors for yourself
even when you seem too tired to go on.
Find the energy to see a new dawn —
a new point of view —
and create a new direction
where none seems possible.
Show your strength and courage
by being optimistic.

≈

Bonnie St. John

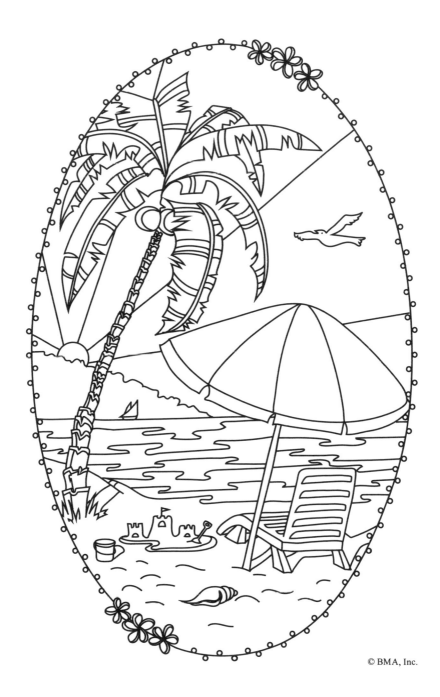

© BMA, Inc.

Think about the good things in life,
like sunshine, holidays, feeling loved,
special friendships, and laughter.
Think about rainbows, blue skies, and
beautiful sunsets and feel loved, cared
about, and accepted. Remember that
in life, although there is some bad stuff,
good things really do happen too.

Maria Mullins

Smile

© BMA, Inc.

Don't let old mistakes or misfortunes hold you down: learn from them, forgive yourself — or others — and move on. Do not be bothered or discouraged by adversity. Instead, meet it as a challenge. Be empowered by the courage it takes you to overcome obstacles. Learn something new every day.

Ashley Rice

Find happiness in nature
in the beauty of a mountain
in the serenity of the sea
Find happiness in friendship
in the fun of doing things together
in the sharing and understanding
Find happiness in your family
in the stability of knowing
      that someone cares
in the strength of love and honesty
Find happiness in yourself
in your mind and body
in your values and achievements
Find happiness in
everything
you
do

—

Susan Polis Schutz

Life is not measured by the number of breaths we take, but by the moments that take our breath away.

— Author Unknown

Stay positive no matter what
is going on in your life.
Life never gives us more
than we can handle,
and you are more than up to the task
of facing whatever challenges
may come your way today.
Just believe in yourself
with everything you've got,
and you will find greatness
in every way, every day.

Ashley Rice

Believe in your own power, your
own potential, and your own
innate goodness.
Every morning, wake with the awe of
just being alive.
Each day, discover the magnificent,
awesome beauty in the world.
Explore and embrace life in yourself
and in everyone you see each day.
Be open to all your possibilities;
possibilities can be miracles.
Believe in miracles!

———

Vickie M. Worsham

Follow your Heart

Seek out that particular mental attribute which makes you feel most deeply and vitally alive, along with which comes the inner voice which says, "This is the real me," and when you have found that attitude, follow it.

William James

Guarantee your peace of mind, contentment, faith, and strength, as well as the constant ability to find joy in all the things that sometimes go unnoticed. Find moments to connect with other individuals who are full of smiles and hugs to give away and stories and laughter to share.

≈

Barbara Cage

The happiest people in the world are those who have a hard time recalling their worries... and an easy time remembering their blessings.

Alin Austin

Find time in each day to see beauty and love in the world around you. Realize that what you feel you lack in one regard may be more than compensated for in another. What you feel you lack in the present may become one of your strengths in the future. See your future filled with promise and possibility. Learn to view everything as a worthwhile experience.

Sandra Sturtz Hauss

Keep
your face to
the sunshine
and you cannot
see the shadow.

≈

Helen Keller

Release the child within you
so you can sing, laugh, and play.
List the things that you do best,
and give yourself a hug.
Accept compliments.
Dance barefoot.
Plan to fulfill a secret wish.
Laugh at yourself.
And above all,
remember you are loved.

~

Jacqueline Schiff

Wake up every day in a good mood
with a smile for the world and a
sunny, easy, and positive attitude,
no matter what the weather is like
or whatever the circumstances. As
you go about your day, take the time
to celebrate yourself and the lives
of those you care about, and realize
how important you are to all those
who know you. Let your last thought
in the evening be one of gratitude
for such a great day.

Donna Fargo

May You
Always
Have
positive
Thoughts

May each new day of your life
bring you fresh hopes for tomorrow
and feelings of excitement, joy, and
a wonderful sense of expectation.

May you remember the good times
and forget the sorrow and pain, for
the good times will remind you of
how special your life has been.

May you always feel secure and
loved and know you are the best.

Above all, may you always have
positive thoughts.

Regina Hill